Traveling the Globe
and Making Memories!

Travel Journal and Scrapbook

Activinotes

Activinotes

DAILY JOURNALS, PLANNERS. NOTEBOOKS AND OTHER BLANK BOOKS

Travel Journal

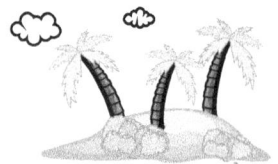

i ♥ Travel

Travel Journal

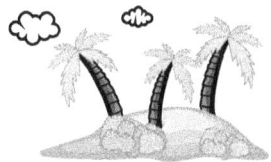

i ♥ Travel

Travel Journal

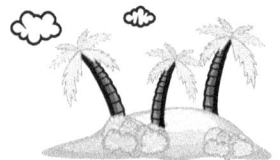

i ♥ Travel

Travel Journal

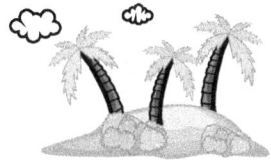

i ♥ Travel

Travel Journal

Travel Journal

i ♥ Travel

Things to See & Do :

- ☐ _____
- ☐ _____
- ☐ _____
- ☐ _____
- ☐ _____
- ☐ _____
- ☐ _____

Things to Observe :

- ☐ ....
- ☐ ....
- ☐ ....
- ☐ ....
- ☐ ....

Adventure to Have :

- ☐ ....
- ☐ ....
- ☐ ....
- ☐ ....
- ☐ ....
- ☐ ....

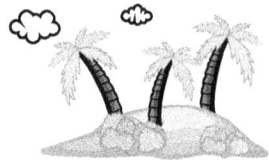

Travel Journal

place your
photo here

Streets to Check Out :

....
- ☐ ....
- ☐ ....
- ☐ ....
- ☐ ....
- ☐ ....
- ☐ ....

PLaces to MingLe :

....
- ☐ ....
- ☐ ....
- ☐ ....
- ☐ ....
- ☐ ....
- ☐ ....

Shops to Visit :

- ☐ _____
- ☐ _____
- ☐ _____
- ☐ _____
- ☐ _____
- ☐ _____
- ☐ _____

   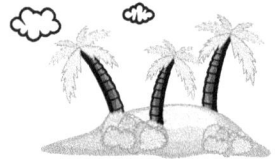

Travel Journal

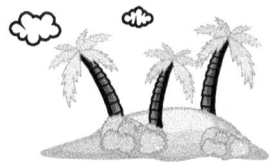

place your
photo here

place your
photo here

place your
photo here

place your
photo here

Travel Journal

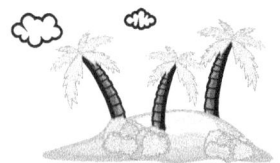

i ❤ Travel

Travel Journal

Travel Journal

i ♥ Travel

Things to See & Do :

- [ ] _____
- [ ] _____
- [ ] _____
- [ ] _____
- [ ] _____
- [ ] _____
- [ ] _____

Things to Observe :

- [ ] ....
- [ ] ....
- [ ] ....
- [ ] ....
- [ ] ....
- [ ] ....

Adventure to Have :

- [ ] ....
- [ ] ....
- [ ] ....
- [ ] ....
- [ ] ....
- [ ] ....

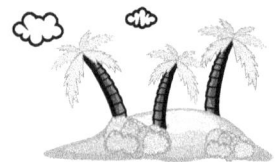

Travel Journal

place your
photo here

Streets to Check Out :

....
☐ ....
☐ ....
☐ ....
☐ ....
☐ ....
☐ ....

PLaces to MingLe :

....
☐ ....
☐ ....
☐ ....
☐ ....
☐ ....
☐ ....

Shops to Visit :

☐ _____
☐ _____
☐ _____
☐ _____
☐ _____
☐ _____
☐ _____

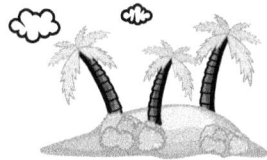

Travel Journal

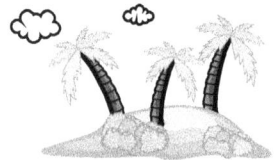

i ♥ Travel

place your
photo here

place your
photo here

place your
photo here

place your
photo here

Travel Journal

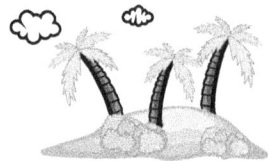

i ♥ Travel

Travel Journal

Travel Journal

Things to See & Do :

- ☐ _____
- ☐ _____
- ☐ _____
- ☐ _____
- ☐ _____
- ☐ _____
- ☐ _____

Things to Observe :

- ☐ ....
- ☐ ....
- ☐ ....
- ☐ ....
- ☐ ....
- ☐ ....

Adventure to Have :

- ☐ ....
- ☐ ....
- ☐ ....
- ☐ ....
- ☐ ....
- ☐ ....

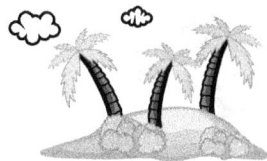

Travel Journal

i ♥ Travel

place your
photo here

Streets to Check Out :

☐ ....
☐ ....
☐ ....
☐ ....
☐ ....
☐ ....

PLaces to MingLe :

☐ ....
☐ ....
☐ ....
☐ ....
☐ ....
☐ ....

Shops to Visit :

☐ _____
☐ _____
☐ _____
☐ _____
☐ _____
☐ _____
☐ _____

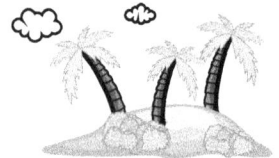

Travel Journal

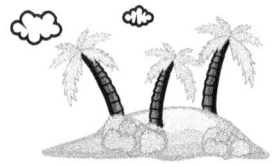

i ♥ Travel

place your photo here

place your photo here

place your photo here

place your photo here

Travel Journal

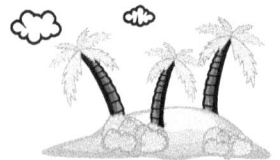

i ♥ Travel

Travel Journal

Travel Journal

i ♥ Travel

Things to See & Do :

- ☐ _____
- ☐ _____
- ☐ _____
- ☐ _____
- ☐ _____
- ☐ _____
- ☐ _____

Things to Observe :

- ☐ ....
- ☐ ....
- ☐ ....
- ☐ ....
- ☐ ....
- ☐ ....

Adventure to Have :

- ☐ ....
- ☐ ....
- ☐ ....
- ☐ ....
- ☐ ....
- ☐ ....

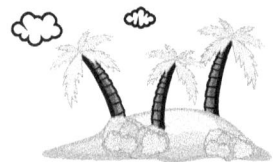

Travel Journal

i ♥ Travel

place your
photo here

Streets to Check Out :

....
☐ ....
☐ ....
☐ ....
☐ ....
☐ ....
☐ ....

Places to MingLe :

....
☐ ....
☐ ....
☐ ....
☐ ....
☐ ....
☐ ....

Shops to Visit :

☐ _____
☐ _____
☐ _____
☐ _____
☐ _____
☐ _____
☐ _____

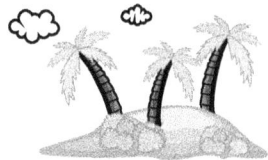

Travel Journal

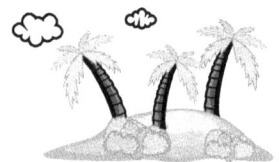

i ♥ Travel

place your
photo here

place your
photo here

place your
photo here

place your
photo here

Travel Journal

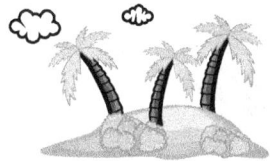

i ❤ Travel

Travel Journal

_____
_____
_____
_____
_____
_____
_____
_____
_____
_____
_____
_____
_____
_____
_____
_____
_____
_____
_____
_____
_____
_____
_____
_____

Travel Journal

Things to See & Do :

- ☐ _____
- ☐ _____
- ☐ _____
- ☐ _____
- ☐ _____
- ☐ _____
- ☐ _____

Things to Observe :

- ☐ ....
- ☐ ....
- ☐ ....
- ☐ ....
- ☐ ....
- ☐ ....

Adventure to Have :

- ☐ ....
- ☐ ....
- ☐ ....
- ☐ ....
- ☐ ....
- ☐ ....

Travel Journal

i ♥ Travel

place your
photo here

Streets to Check Out :

....
- ☐ ....
- ☐ ....
- ☐ ....
- ☐ ....
- ☐ ....
- ☐ ....

Places to Mingle :

....
- ☐ ....
- ☐ ....
- ☐ ....
- ☐ ....
- ☐ ....
- ☐ ....

Shops to Visit :

- ☐ _____
- ☐ _____
- ☐ _____
- ☐ _____
- ☐ _____
- ☐ _____
- ☐ _____

Travel Journal

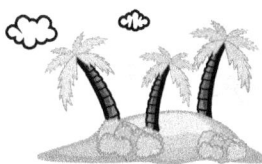

i ♥ Travel

place your
photo here

place your
photo here

place your
photo here

place your
photo here

Travel Journal

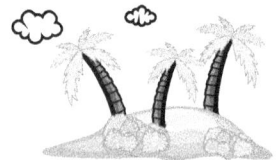

Travel Journal

i ❤ Travel

Travel Journal

Things to See & Do :

- ☐ _____
- ☐ _____
- ☐ _____
- ☐ _____
- ☐ _____
- ☐ _____
- ☐ _____

Things to Observe :

- ☐ _____
- ☐ _____
- ☐ _____
- ☐ _____
- ☐ _____
- ☐ _____

Adventure to Have :

- ☐ _____
- ☐ _____
- ☐ _____
- ☐ _____
- ☐ _____
- ☐ _____

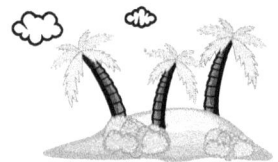

Travel Journal

place your
photo here

Streets to Check Out :

....
☐ ....
☐ ....
☐ ....
☐ ....
☐ ....
☐ ....

PLaces to MingLe :

....
☐ ....
☐ ....
☐ ....
☐ ....
☐ ....
☐ ....

Shops to Visit :

☐ _____
☐ _____
☐ _____
☐ _____
☐ _____
☐ _____
☐ _____

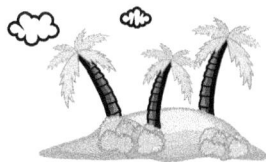

Travel Journal

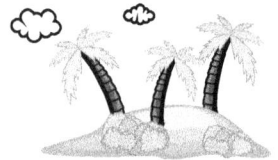

i ♥ Travel

place your
photo here

place your
photo here

place your
photo here

place your
photo here

Travel Journal

i ❤ Travel

Travel Journal

_____
_____
_____
_____
_____
_____
_____
_____
_____
_____
_____
_____
_____
_____
_____
_____
_____
_____
_____
_____
_____
_____
_____
_____

Travel Journal

i ♡ Travel

Things to See & Do :

- ☐ _____
- ☐ _____
- ☐ _____
- ☐ _____
- ☐ _____
- ☐ _____
- ☐ _____

Things to Observe :

- ☐ ....
- ☐ ....
- ☐ ....
- ☐ ....
- ☐ ....
- ☐ ....

Adventure to Have :

- ☐ ....
- ☐ ....
- ☐ ....
- ☐ ....
- ☐ ....
- ☐ ....

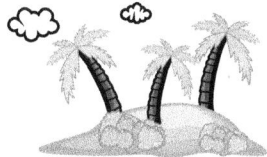

Travel Journal

i ♥ Travel

place your photo here

Streets to Check Out :

☐ ....
☐ ....
☐ ....
☐ ....
☐ ....
☐ ....

PLaces to MingLe :

☐ ....
☐ ....
☐ ....
☐ ....
☐ ....
☐ ....

Shops to Visit :

☐ _____
☐ _____
☐ _____
☐ _____
☐ _____
☐ _____
☐ _____

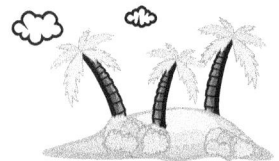

Travel Journal

i ♥ Travel

place your
photo here

place your
photo here

place your
photo here

place your
photo here

Travel Journal

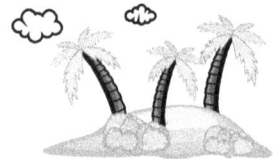

i ♥ Travel

Travel Journal

Travel Journal

i
❤
Travel

Things to See & Do :

- ☐ _____
- ☐ _____
- ☐ _____
- ☐ _____
- ☐ _____
- ☐ _____
- ☐ _____

Things to Observe :

- ☐ ....
- ☐ ....
- ☐ ....
- ☐ ....
- ☐ ....
- ☐ ....

Adventure to Have :

- ☐ ....
- ☐ ....
- ☐ ....
- ☐ ....
- ☐ ....
- ☐ ....

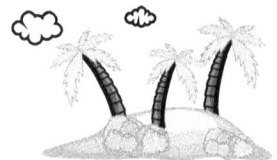

Travel Journal

place your
photo here

Streets to Check Out :

....
- [ ] ....
- [ ] ....
- [ ] ....
- [ ] ....
- [ ] ....
- [ ] ....

PLaces to MingLe :

....
- [ ] ....
- [ ] ....
- [ ] ....
- [ ] ....
- [ ] ....
- [ ] ....

Shops to Visit :

- [ ] _____
- [ ] _____
- [ ] _____
- [ ] _____
- [ ] _____
- [ ] _____
- [ ] _____

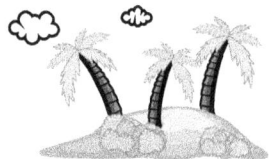

Travel Journal

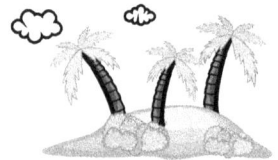

i ♥ Travel

place your
photo here

place your
photo here

place your
photo here

place your
photo here

Travel Journal

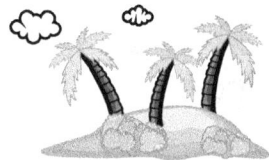

i ♥ Travel

Travel Journal

_____
_____
_____
_____
_____
_____
_____
_____
_____
_____
_____
_____
_____
_____
_____
_____
_____
_____
_____
_____
_____
_____
_____

Travel Journal

i ♥ Travel

Things to See & Do :

- [ ] _____
- [ ] _____
- [ ] _____
- [ ] _____
- [ ] _____
- [ ] _____
- [ ] _____

Things to Observe :

- [ ] ....
- [ ] ....
- [ ] ....
- [ ] ....
- [ ] ....
- [ ] ....

Adventure to Have :

- [ ] ....
- [ ] ....
- [ ] ....
- [ ] ....
- [ ] ....
- [ ] ....

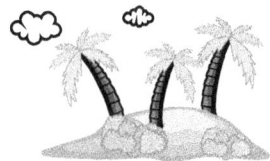

Travel Journal

i ♥ Travel

place your
photo here

Streets to Check Out :

....
☐ ....
☐ ....
☐ ....
☐ ....
☐ ....
☐ ....

PLaces to MingLe :

....
☐ ....
☐ ....
☐ ....
☐ ....
☐ ....
☐ ....

Shops to Visit :

☐ _____
☐ _____
☐ _____
☐ _____
☐ _____
☐ _____
☐ _____

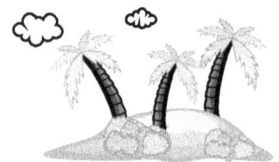

Travel Journal

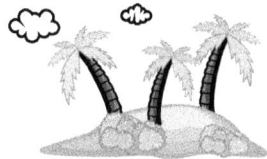

i ♥ Travel

place your photo here

place your photo here

place your photo here

place your photo here

Travel Journal

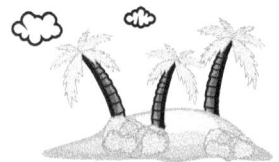

i ❤ Travel

Travel Journal

Travel Journal

i ♥ Travel

Things to See & Do :

☐ _____
☐ _____
☐ _____
☐ _____
☐ _____
☐ _____
☐ _____

Things to Observe :

☐ ....
☐ ....
☐ ....
☐ ....
☐ ....
☐ ....

Adventure to Have :

☐ ....
☐ ....
☐ ....
☐ ....
☐ ....
☐ ....

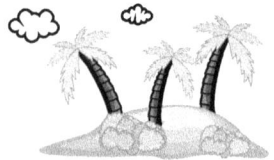

Travel Journal

i ♥ Travel

place your
photo here

Streets to Check Out :

....
☐ ....
☐ ....
☐ ....
☐ ....
☐ ....
☐ ....

PLaces to MingLe :

....
☐ ....
☐ ....
☐ ....
☐ ....
☐ ....
☐ ....

Shops to Visit :

☐ _____
☐ _____
☐ _____
☐ _____
☐ _____
☐ _____
☐ _____

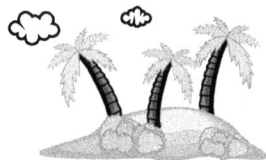

Travel Journal

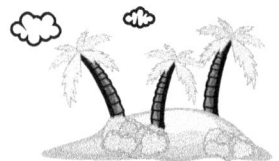

place your
photo here

place your
photo here

place your
photo here

place your
photo here

Travel Journal

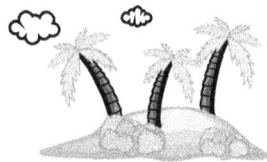

Travel Journal

i ❤ Travel

Travel Journal

Things to See & Do :

- ☐ _____
- ☐ _____
- ☐ _____
- ☐ _____
- ☐ _____
- ☐ _____
- ☐ _____

Things to Observe :

- ☐ ....
- ☐ ....
- ☐ ....
- ☐ ....
- ☐ ....
- ☐ ....

Adventure to Have :

- ☐ ....
- ☐ ....
- ☐ ....
- ☐ ....
- ☐ ....
- ☐ ....

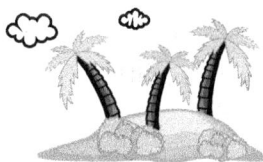

Travel Journal

i ♥ Travel

place your
photo here

Streets to Check Out :

....
☐ ....
☐ ....
☐ ....
☐ ....
☐ ....
☐ ....

PLaces to MingLe :

....
☐ ....
☐ ....
☐ ....
☐ ....
☐ ....
☐ ....

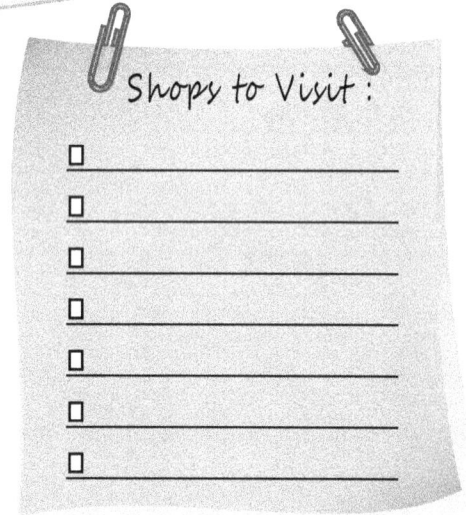

Shops to Visit :

☐ _____
☐ _____
☐ _____
☐ _____
☐ _____
☐ _____
☐ _____

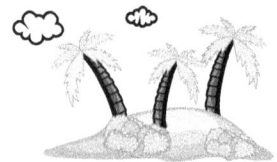

Travel Journal

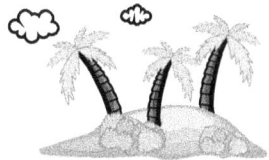

i ♥ Travel

place your
photo here

place your
photo here

place your
photo here

place your
photo here

Travel Journal

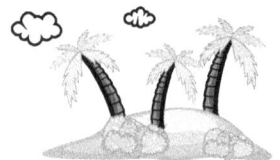

i ♥ Travel

Travel Journal

I ❤ Travel

Travel Journal

Things to See & Do :

- [ ] _____
- [ ] _____
- [ ] _____
- [ ] _____
- [ ] _____
- [ ] _____
- [ ] _____

Things to Observe :

- [ ] ....
- [ ] ....
- [ ] ....
- [ ] ....
- [ ] ....
- [ ] ....

Adventure to Have :

- [ ] ....
- [ ] ....
- [ ] ....
- [ ] ....
- [ ] ....
- [ ] ....

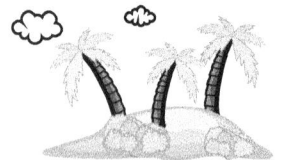

Travel Journal

place your
photo here

Streets to Check Out :

....
☐ ....
☐ ....
☐ ....
☐ ....
☐ ....
☐ ....

PLaces to MingLe :

....
☐ ....
☐ ....
☐ ....
☐ ....
☐ ....
☐ ....

Shops to Visit :

☐ _____
☐ _____
☐ _____
☐ _____
☐ _____
☐ _____
☐ _____

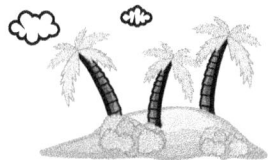

Travel Journal

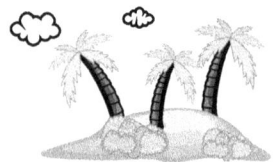

i ♥ Travel

place your
photo here

place your
photo here

place your
photo here

place your
photo here

Travel Journal

i ♥ Travel

Travel Journal

_____
_____
_____
_____
_____
_____
_____
_____
_____
_____
_____
_____
_____
_____
_____
_____
_____
_____
_____
_____
_____
_____
_____
_____
_____

Travel Journal

Things to See & Do :

- ☐ _____
- ☐ _____
- ☐ _____
- ☐ _____
- ☐ _____
- ☐ _____
- ☐ _____

Things to Observe :

- ☐ ....
- ☐ ....
- ☐ ....
- ☐ ....
- ☐ ....
- ☐ ....

Adventure to Have :

- ☐ ....
- ☐ ....
- ☐ ....
- ☐ ....
- ☐ ....
- ☐ ....

Travel Journal

place your
photo here

Streets to Check Out :

....
☐ ....
☐ ....
☐ ....
☐ ....
☐ ....
☐ ....

PLaces to MingLe :

....
☐ ....
☐ ....
☐ ....
☐ ....
☐ ....
☐

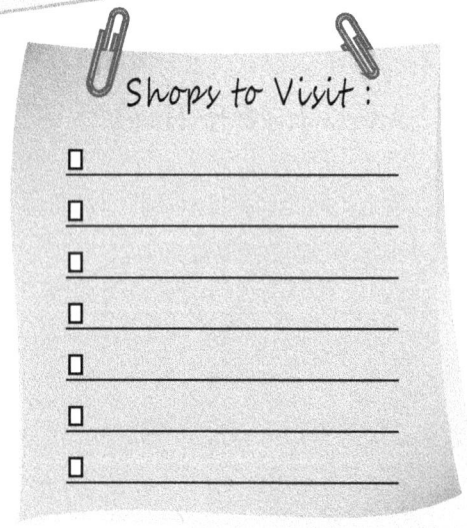

Shops to Visit :

☐ _____
☐ _____
☐ _____
☐ _____
☐ _____
☐ _____
☐ _____

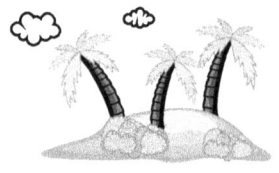

Travel Journal

i ♥ Travel

place your photo here

place your photo here

place your photo here

place your photo here

Travel Journal

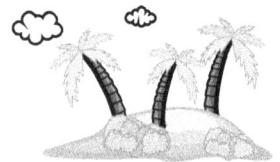

i ♥ Travel

Travel Journal

_____
_____
_____
_____
_____
_____
_____
_____
_____
_____
_____
_____
_____
_____
_____
_____
_____
_____
_____
_____
_____
_____
_____
_____
_____

Travel Journal

i ♥ Travel

Things to See & Do :

- ☐ _____
- ☐ _____
- ☐ _____
- ☐ _____
- ☐ _____
- ☐ _____
- ☐ _____

Things to Observe :

- ☐ ....
- ☐ ....
- ☐ ....
- ☐ ....
- ☐ ....

Adventure to Have :

- ☐ ....
- ☐ ....
- ☐ ....
- ☐ ....
- ☐ ....

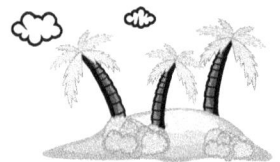

Travel Journal

place your
photo here

Streets to Check Out :

....
☐ ....
☐ ....
☐ ....
☐ ....
☐ ....
☐ ....

PLaces to MingLe :

....
☐ ....
☐ ....
☐ ....
☐ ....
☐ ....
☐ ....

Shops to Visit :

☐ _____
☐ _____
☐ _____
☐ _____
☐ _____
☐ _____
☐ _____

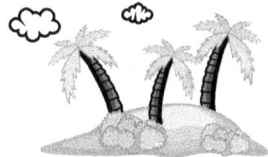

Travel Journal

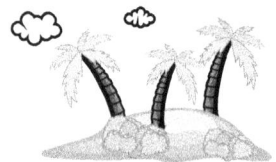

i ♥ Travel

place your
photo here

place your
photo here

place your
photo here

place your
photo here

Travel Journal

i ♥ Travel

Travel Journal

i love Travel

Travel Journal

Things to See & Do :

- ☐ _____
- ☐ _____
- ☐ _____
- ☐ _____
- ☐ _____
- ☐ _____
- ☐ _____

Things to Observe :

- ☐ ....
- ☐ ....
- ☐ ....
- ☐ ....
- ☐ ....
- ☐ ....

Adventure to Have :

- ☐ ....
- ☐ ....
- ☐ ....
- ☐ ....
- ☐ ....
- ☐ ....

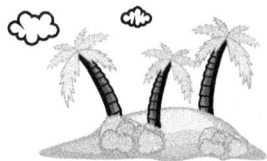

Travel Journal

place your
photo here

Streets to Check Out :

☐ ....
☐ ....
☐ ....
☐ ....
☐ ....
☐ ....

PLaces to MingLe :

☐ ....
☐ ....
☐ ....
☐ ....
☐ ....
☐ ....

Shops to Visit :

☐ _____
☐ _____
☐ _____
☐ _____
☐ _____
☐ _____
☐ _____

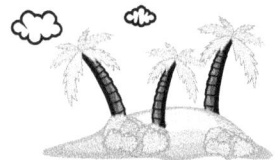

Travel Journal

i ♥ Travel

place your
photo here

place your
photo here

place your
photo here

place your
photo here

Travel Journal

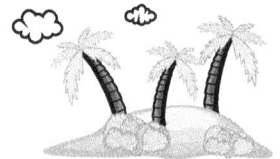

Travel Journal

_____
_____
_____
_____
_____
_____
_____
_____
_____
_____
_____
_____
_____
_____
_____
_____
_____
_____
_____
_____
_____
_____
_____

Travel Journal

i ♥ Travel

Things to See & Do :

- [ ] _____
- [ ] _____
- [ ] _____
- [ ] _____
- [ ] _____
- [ ] _____
- [ ] _____

Things to Observe :

- [ ] ....
- [ ] ....
- [ ] ....
- [ ] ....
- [ ] ....
- [ ] ....

Adventure to Have :

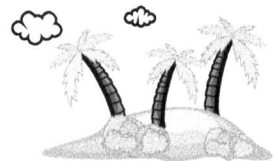

- [ ] ....
- [ ] ....
- [ ] ....
- [ ] ....
- [ ] ....
- [ ] ....

Travel Journal

place your
photo here

Streets to Check Out :

....
☐ ....
☐ ....
☐ ....
☐ ....
☐ ....
☐ ....

PLaces to MingLe :

....
☐ ....
☐ ....
☐ ....
☐ ....
☐ ....
☐ ....

Shops to Visit :

☐ _____
☐ _____
☐ _____
☐ _____
☐ _____
☐ _____
☐ _____

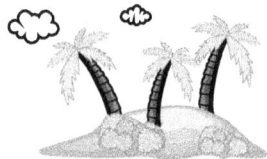

Travel Journal

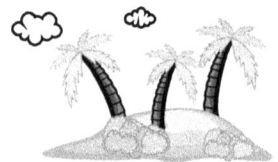

i ♥ Travel

place your
photo here

place your
photo here

place your
photo here

place your
photo here

Travel Journal

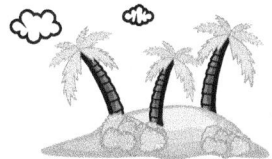

Travel Journal

Travel Journal

Things to See & Do :

- ☐ _____
- ☐ _____
- ☐ _____
- ☐ _____
- ☐ _____
- ☐ _____
- ☐ _____

Things to Observe :

- ☐ ....
- ☐ ....
- ☐ ....
- ☐ ....
- ☐ ....
- ☐ ....

Adventure to Have :

- ☐ ....
- ☐ ....
- ☐ ....
- ☐ ....
- ☐ ....
- ☐ ....

Travel Journal

place your
photo here

Streets to Check Out :

....
☐ ....
☐ ....
☐ ....
☐ ....
☐ ....
☐ ....

Places to Mingle :

....
☐ ....
☐ ....
☐ ....
☐ ....
☐ ....
☐ ....

Shops to Visit :

☐ _____
☐ _____
☐ _____
☐ _____
☐ _____
☐ _____
☐ _____

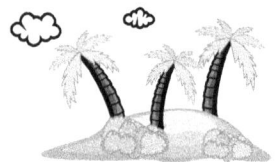

Travel Journal

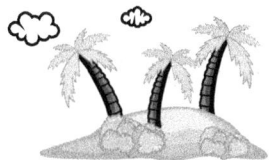

i ♥ Travel

place your photo here

place your photo here

place your photo here

place your photo here

Travel Journal

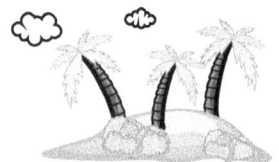

i ♥ Travel

Travel Journal

Travel Journal

i ❤ Travel

Things to See & Do :

- ☐ _____
- ☐ _____
- ☐ _____
- ☐ _____
- ☐ _____
- ☐ _____
- ☐ _____

Things to Observe :

- ☐ ....
- ☐ ....
- ☐ ....
- ☐ ....
- ☐ ....
- ☐ ....

Adventure to Have :

- ☐ ....
- ☐ ....
- ☐ ....
- ☐ ....
- ☐ ....
- ☐ ....

Travel Journal

place your
photo here

Streets to Check Out :

- ☐ ....
- ☐ ....
- ☐ ....
- ☐ ....
- ☐ ....
- ☐ ....

PLaces to MingLe :

- ☐ ....
- ☐ ....
- ☐ ....
- ☐ ....
- ☐ ....
- ☐ ....

Shops to Visit :

- ☐ _____
- ☐ _____
- ☐ _____
- ☐ _____
- ☐ _____
- ☐ _____
- ☐ _____

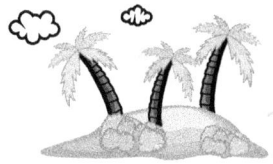

Travel Journal

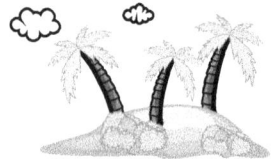

i ♥ Travel

place your
photo here

place your
photo here

place your
photo here

place your
photo here

Travel Journal

i ♥ Travel

Travel Journal

Travel Journal

Things to See & Do :

- ☐ _____
- ☐ _____
- ☐ _____
- ☐ _____
- ☐ _____
- ☐ _____
- ☐ _____

Things to Observe :

- ☐ ....
- ☐ ....
- ☐ ....
- ☐ ....
- ☐ ....
- ☐ ....

Adventure to Have :

- ☐ ....
- ☐ ....
- ☐ ....
- ☐ ....
- ☐ ....
- ☐ ....

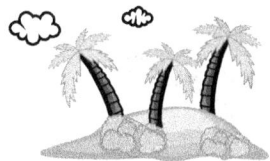

Travel Journal

place your
photo here

Streets to Check Out :

....
☐ ....
☐ ....
☐ ....
☐ ....
☐ ....
☐ ....

PLaces to MingLe :

....
☐ ....
☐ ....
☐ ....
☐ ....
☐ ....
☐ ....

Shops to Visit :

☐ _____
☐ _____
☐ _____
☐ _____
☐ _____
☐ _____
☐ _____

Travel Journal

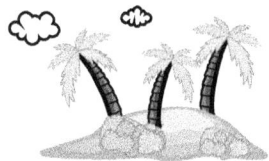

i ♥ Travel

place your
photo here

place your
photo here

place your
photo here

place your
photo here

Travel Journal

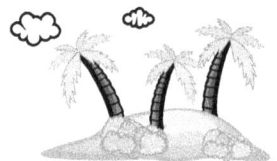

Travel Journal

i ♥ Travel

Travel Journal

i love Travel

Things to See & Do :

- [ ] _____
- [ ] _____
- [ ] _____
- [ ] _____
- [ ] _____
- [ ] _____
- [ ] _____

Things to Observe :

- [ ] _____
- [ ] _____
- [ ] _____
- [ ] _____
- [ ] _____
- [ ] _____

Adventure to Have :

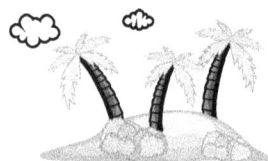

- [ ] _____
- [ ] _____
- [ ] _____
- [ ] _____
- [ ] _____
- [ ] _____

Travel Journal

place your
photo here

Streets to Check Out :

....
☐ ....
☐ ....
☐ ....
☐ ....
☐ ....
☐ ....

Shops to Visit :

☐ _____
☐ _____
☐ _____
☐ _____
☐ _____
☐ _____
☐ _____

PLaces to MingLe :

....
☐ ....
☐ ....
☐ ....
☐ ....
☐ ....
☐ ....

Travel Journal

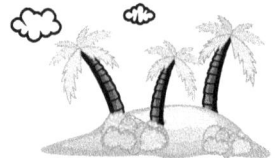

i ♥ Travel

place your
photo here

place your
photo here

place your
photo here

place your
photo here

Travel Journal

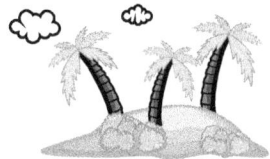

www.ingramcontent.com/pod-product-compliance
Lightning Source LLC
Chambersburg PA
CBHW081338090426

42737CB00017B/3197